DISCOVERING

ANCIENT CIVILIZATIONS

THE ANCIENT GREEKS

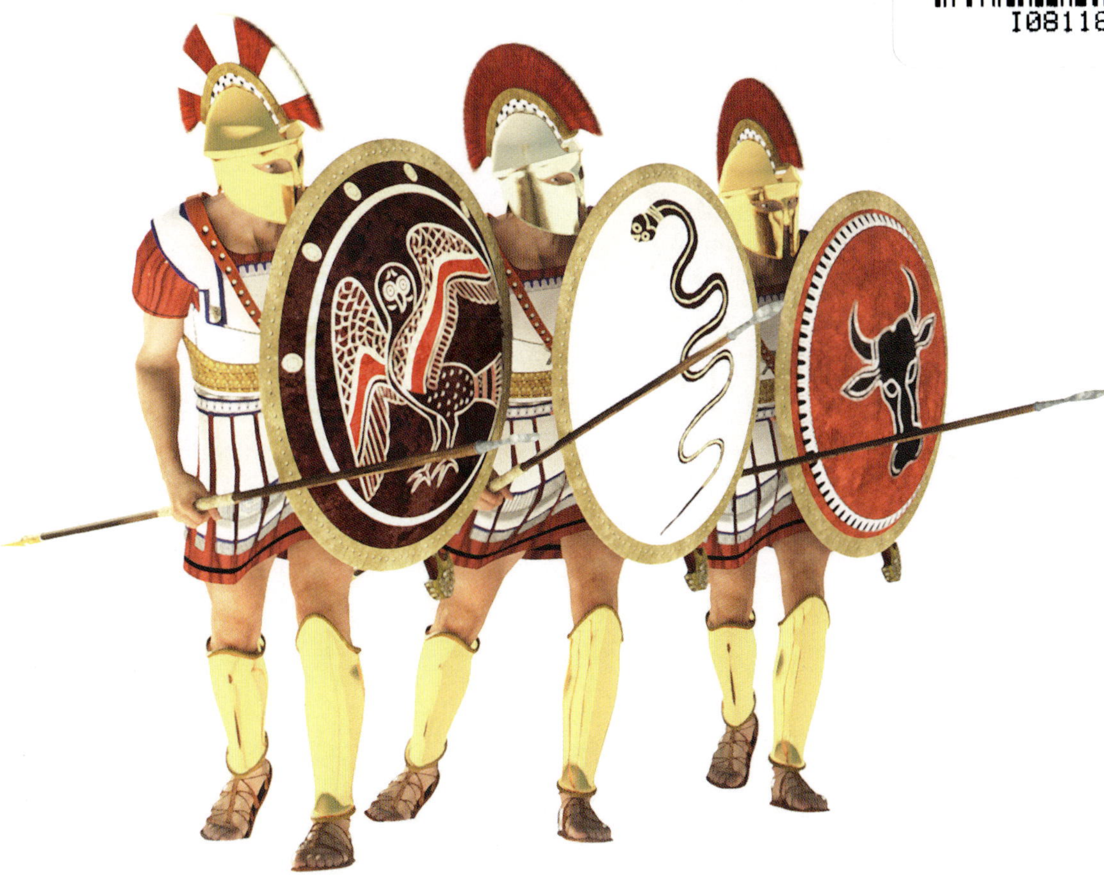

David West

Gareth Stevens
PUBLISHING

Please visit our website, www.garethstevens.com.
For a free color catalog of all our high-quality books,
call toll free 1-800-542-2595 or fax 1-877-542-2596.

Cataloging-in-Publication Data

Names: West, David.
Title: The ancient Greeks / David West.
Description: New York : Gareth Stevens Publishing, 2017. | Series: Discovering ancient civilizations | Includes index.
Identifiers: ISBN 9781482450637 (pbk.) | ISBN 9781482450651 (library bound) | ISBN 9781482450644 (6 pack)
Subjects: LCSH: Greeks–Social life and customs–Juvenile literature. | Greece–History–To 146 B.C.–Juvenile literature.
Classification: LCC DF77.W47 2017 | DDC 938–dc23

First Edition

Published in 2017 by
Gareth Stevens Publishing
111 East 14th Street, Suite 349
New York, NY 10003

Designed by David West Books

Printed in the United States of America
CPSIA compliance information: Batch #CS16GS: For further information contact Gareth Stevens, New York, New York at 1-800-542-2595.

DISCOVERING
ANCIENT CIVILIZATIONS

THE ANCIENT GREEKS

David West

Gareth Stevens
PUBLISHING

CONTENTS

Ancient Greece Lasted 1,000 Years

Ancient Greece is the term used to describe the Greek-speaking world in ancient times. This included many areas along the coast of the Mediterranean and Black Seas. It was made up of several hundred city-states (poleis), which shared the same religion, culture, and language.

Its history is divided into four periods: the Greek Dark Ages (1100–800 BC), the Archaic Period (800–500 BC), the Classical Years (500–323 BC), and the Hellenistic Years which followed the conquests of Alexander the Great (323–146 BC).

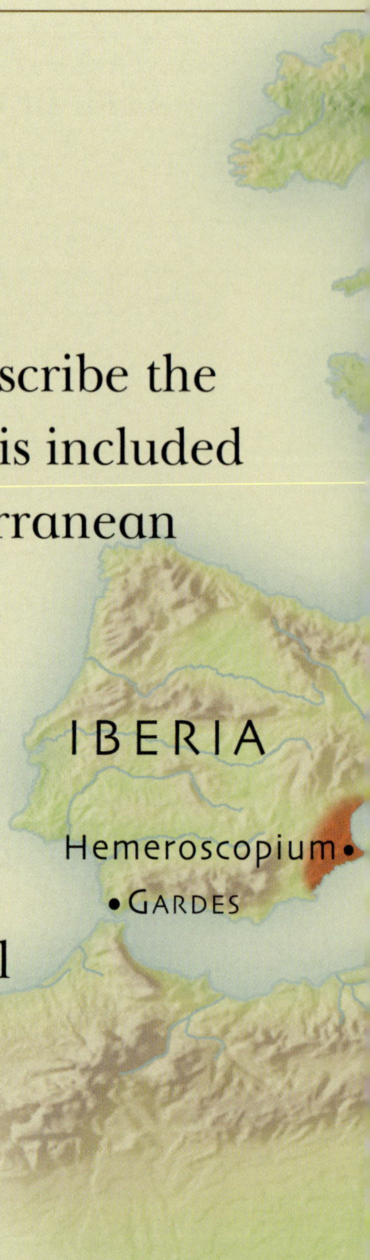

The red areas show the ancient Greek-speaking world at around 550 BC. From about 750 BC the Greeks began 250 years of expansion, settling colonies in all directions.

Only free, landowning, native-born men could be citizens in a city-state. In most poleis the rich aristocracy usually ruled. Athens founded the world's first ***democracy*** *which allowed its citizens equal privileges. This did not include women or slaves. Many other poleis followed this example, but not all of them.*

THE ANCIENT GREEKS HAD A GOOD DIET

Along the coasts, fresh fish and seafood were available. Eggs, milk, cheese, and yogurt were eaten although butter was not. Vegetables such as asparagus, fennel, cucumbers, chickpeas, onions, lentils, and celery were grown. They were often eaten in soups. Poor families ate acorns. Bread, honey, olives, fruits, and nuts were also a large part of the Greek diet.

A farmer and his son take a donkey loaded with produce to the market. They pass peasants knocking olives from trees and a distant vineyard.

Ancient Greeks didn't eat much meat. In the country, birds and hares were trapped. Peasants kept chickens and geese. Wealthy landowners raised goats, pigs, and sheep.

The Spartans mainly ate a pork stew, called "black broth." The dish was served with ***maza****, figs, and cheese.*

ANCIENT GREEKS WERE GREAT TRADERS

Ancient Greece had thousands of miles of coastline which allowed them to trade far and wide by sea. For this they built specialized merchant ships. Goods traded within Greece between the different poleis included cereals, wine, olives, figs, peas and beans, cheese, honey, meat, perfumes, and pottery.

They exported pottery, wine, olive oil, and marble.

A merchant greets his ship's captain as it is unloaded with produce including many ***amphorae*** *of olive oil and wine.*

Imports included wheat and slaves from Egypt, grain from the Black Sea, wood from Macedonia, papyrus, textiles, spices, glass, iron, copper, tin, gold, and silver from around the Mediterranean Sea.

Disagreements between the city-states sometimes ended in embargoes enforced by navy ***triremes****.*

A CITY'S CENTER WAS CALLED THE AGORA

Each city-state had a central square where people gathered to hear important announcements, to muster for military campaigns, and to discuss politics. It was also where the main tented market was situated. The agora of Athens had slave traders, pastry and sweet makers, wine merchants, fishmongers, cloth merchants, shoemakers,

A market in a city-state's agora sells food, clothes, and pottery. In the background long colonnades called stoa contain shops and offices.

dressmakers, and jewelry craftsmen. The **philosophers Socrates** and **Plato** were often found talking to merchants in the Athenian agora.

The philosopher Diogenes of Sinope lived in a large wine cask in the agora of Athens.

ONLY WEALTHY BOYS WENT TO SCHOOL

In most poleis schools were small with only one teacher and between ten to 20 students. The schools were not free so only wealthy citizens could afford to educate their boys. The schoolroom had no desks. Boys wrote on a wax-covered wooden board with a wooden stick called a stylus.

Boys started school at seven years old, and learned

Pupils in an ancient Greek school write on wax tablets as their tutor looks on. A slave in the background maintains discipline.

reading, writing, arithmetic, music, and poetry. In the afternoons they practiced sports such as wrestling, running, and throwing the javelin. It was important to grow up strong and fit for military service.

Girls were taught at home by their mothers. They learned housework, cooking, and skills such as weaving.

IT WAS TOUGH BEING A SPARTAN

Boys in **Sparta** were taken from their families at seven years old and sent to army school. Here they were allowed one tunic a year and had to walk barefoot. They were taught how to fight and encouraged to steal. As well as training, boys studied reading, writing, music, and dancing. They were often punished with beatings that could sometimes kill a boy.

*Two Spartan boys steal fruit from a **helot**'s market stall as hoplites and others look on without surprise.*

At the age of 20 they became soldiers and served until they were 30. They could get married at 20 but still had to live in barracks until they left the army.

Spartan girls also did physical exercise. A Spartan woman had more freedom than other Greek women. She ran her husband's farm and was in charge of the helot slaves.

Ancient Greeks worshiped many gods

The ancient Greeks prayed to the gods both at home and as they went about their daily business. If they wanted a favor from a particular god they would go to that god's temple and make a sacrifice. A priest ensured the sacrifice was made correctly. Different gods helped in different ways. Asclepius, for example, was the god of medicine and

Visitors wait for priests to interpret the oracle's prophecies as she sits in a trance on a tripod. Fumes rising from cracks in the floor surround her.

people would pray to him if they were ill.

People never started anything important without learning what the gods thought. So they visited a soothsayer who could foresee the future or an **oracle** who spoke on behalf of a god.

Zeus was the ruler of the gods. He lived on Mount Olympus.

ANCIENT GREEK THEATER LASTED ALL DAY

Theater in ancient Greece developed from a religious festival held in honor of the god **Dionysus**. Later it became a more formal event and special open-air theaters were built that could hold 18,000 people. The theaters were built into a hillside and were designed so that the people sitting at the top could hear just as clearly as those at the bottom.

In an ancient Greek theater people watch the chorus sing and dance in a circular area, called the orchestra, which was in front of the stage.

The audience watched several plays which lasted all day. There were two types of plays, tragedies and comedies. Often playwrights competed against each other with poems, songs, and plays.

All the performers were men. They wore bright clothes and very expressive masks.

The Olympic Games Started in Greece

The Olympic Games began in 776 BC. They were a series of athletic competitions held every four years in Olympia. They were part of religious celebrations held in honor of Zeus. People from all over the Greek world traveled to watch and take part. At times of war a truce was held during the games so that athletes could travel to the games in safety.

Competitors in the hoplitodromos (hoplite race), wearing helmets and carrying shields, sprint pass spectators who sit at the trackside.

Only young men could compete and no women were allowed to attend the games. Events included wrestling, boxing, long jump, javelin, discus, and chariot racing. The last and toughest event was the hoplite race.

Artistic competitions also featured in the Olympics. Sculptors and poets displayed their works of art to visitors.

ANCIENT GREEKS WERE LOVERS OF KNOWLEDGE

Ancient Greek scholars were some of the first people in history to question how our world worked. They were called philosophers, which means "lovers of knowledge." As well as **philosophy** they studied many subjects including biology, mathematics, astronomy, and geography.

Pythagoras, **Euclid**, and **Archimedes** worked out many

Archimedes tests a prototype of his new invention for raising water to help irrigate fields. It is known today as the Archimedes' screw.

rules of mathematics that we still use today. Thales of Miletus could calculate the height of an Egyptian pyramid by measuring its shadow.

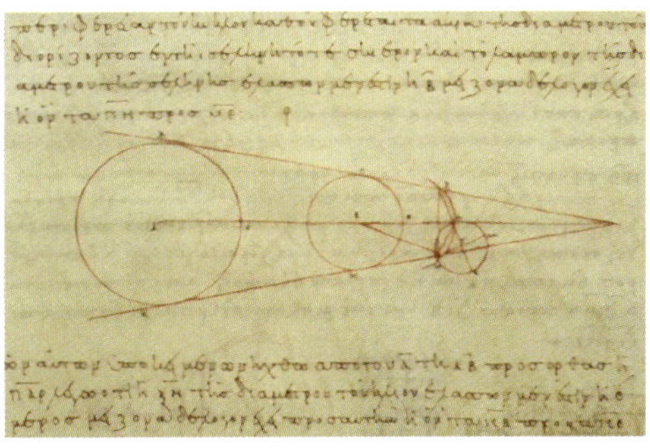

The astronomer Aristarchus worked out that Earth revolved on its axis and went around the sun. Few people believed him since he could not provide evidence to prove it.

GREEK SOLDIERS WERE CALLED HOPLITES

Hoplites were heavily armed infantry in ancient Greece. Most Greek city-states did not have professional armies. Citizens had to equip themselves with weapons and armor. Male citizens up to the age of 60 could be called up to fight in a war.

A hoplite's weapons were a long, iron-tipped, wooden spear and a short sword. A bronze helmet with a crest

A hoplite phalanx, eight rows deep, advances toward the enemy. The large shields were often decorated with colorful designs.

protected the head. Body protection was armor made from laminated linen. Bronze greaves covered the shins. Each hoplite carried a large shield called a hoplon.

Much of ancient Greece's history is blighted by wars between the poleis. When the Persians invaded, poleis grouped together to fight them.

THE ROMANS TOOK OVER THE GREEK WORLD

After centuries of conflict between the city-states a final battle at Mantinea (362 BC) left their armies weakened. This allowed the Macedonians, under Philip II, to invade the Greek city-states and defeat them. He made all the city-states, except Sparta, join together under his leadership.

Massed ranks of a Macedonian army's infantry and cavalry, under the leadership of Philip II, invade a Greek city-state.

When Philip II was assassinated in 336 BC, his son Alexander continued expanding the Macedonian empire. When Alexander died in 323 BC, Greek power was at its greatest. It reached as far west as the Indus River and included Persia and Egypt.

Greece eventually came under the rule of the Roman Republic in 146 BC.

GLOSSARY

amphora (plural: amphorae)
A two-handled pot with a narrow neck used to store wine and olive oil.

Archimedes
An ancient Greek mathematician, physicist, engineer, inventor, and astronomer.

democracy
A system of government of a country (or city-state) by representatives elected by the citizens.

Dionysus
The ancient Greek god of the grape harvest, wine making and wine, and revelry, fertility, and theater. He is often shown with grape vines.

Euclid
An ancient Greek mathematician, often referred to as the "father of geometry." His *Elements* was the main textbook for teaching mathematics (especially geometry) from 300 BC until the late 19th century.

helots
The original inhabitants of Laconia (the area around the Spartan capital) who, after its conquest, became enslaved by the Spartans.

maza
Barley-cake which was a basic ingredient in the ancient Greek diet. It could also be a type of simple bread or pancake made from barley.

oracle
A person who provides information or prophecies of the future, inspired by the gods. It is also the place where the message is given or the message itself.

philosopher
Someone who studies philosophy (see below). In ancient Greece the term was used to describe anyone who studied any of the sciences.

philosophy
The study of the nature of knowledge, reality, and existence.

Plato
A Greek philosopher and mathematician who founded the Academy in Athens—the first institution of higher learning in the Western world.

Pythagoras
An ancient Greek mathematician and scientist best known for the Pythagorean theorem still taught in schools today.

Socrates
An ancient Greek philosopher who was one of the founders of Western philosophy (*see above*).

Sparta
A city-state in ancient Greece renowned for its military power.

trireme
A warship used by the Phoenicians, ancient Greeks, and Romans that had sails and three banks of oars. It also had a metal ram on the front at sea level which was used to smash into the hulls of enemy ships.

INDEX

FOR MORE INFORMATION

BOOKS

Saxon, Liam. *A Smart Kids Guide to Ancient Greek Gods and Goddesses and Ancient Greek Mythology*. Seattle: CreateSpace Independent, 2015.

Macdonald, Fiona. *Ancient Greece*. New York: Barnes & Noble, 2013.

WEBSITES

Ancient Greece
greece.mrdonn.org

History for Kids – Guide to Ancient Greece
www.historyforkids.net/ancient-greece.html

Publisher's note to educators and parents: Our editors have carefully reviewed these websites to ensure that they are suitable for students. Many websites change frequently, however, and we cannot guarantee that a site's future contents will continue to meet our high standards of quality and educational value. Be advised that students should be closely supervised whenever they access the Internet.